ORDER BOOKS - DIRECT

We're <u>faster</u> and <u>cheaper</u> than bookstores!

Please check <u>which</u> book you are ordering:

Quantity	Book Title	Total Cost Per Book (Tax & shipping included)
_____	**ATTENTION DEFICIT DISORDER** A common but often over- looked disorder of Children ISBN 0-9619650-0-2	$11.95
_____	**UNFULFILLED POTENTIAL** The ADD Child as an Adult ISBN 0-9619650-1-0	$11.95
_____	**WHY ADD IS OVERLOOKED & MISUNDERSTOOD** (And reasons this will continue) ISBN 0-9619650-3-7	$4.95
_____	**THE 12 CATEGORIES OF ADD** A classification system for Children, Teens, and Adults ISBN 0-9619650-2-9	$6.95

Send check or money order to FORRESST PUBLISHING, P.O. Box 155774, Fort Worth, TX 76155-0774

Watch for other books to be released by Mr. Hunsucker.

NAME: _____

ADDRESS: _____

CITY: _____ STATE: _____ ZIP: _____

(In Canada or outside the continental U.S., price will vary because of taxes and shipping.)

12 Categories of A.D.D.

ABOUT THE CATEGORIES

1. The categories are separated by age groups.

   a. Child Categories
   b. Teen Categories
   c. Adult Categories

2. Each age group has 4 categories.

   Category I   - Classic ADD
   Category II - Semi-Classic ADD
   Category III - Semi-Complex ADD
   Category IV - Complex ADD

Brief Description of Each Category

Here is an over-simplified description of each category.

Category I
Classic ADD   Behavior Problems

Category II
Semi-Classic ADD   Academic & Behavior Problems

Category III
Semi-Complex ADD   Academic Problems

Category IV
Complex ADD   Emotional Problems and/or
                               Academic & Behavior Problems

Child
Categories

Child Category I

(Classic)

This category is the most easily recognized.

The symptoms and traits of this category correspond to what is commonly called ADD with hyperactivity.

For years, ADD was thought to consist of only the symptoms that were easily observed.

The symptoms in this category are primarily behavioral. Therefore, they are easily recognized by casual observation. Very little testing is required to determine the presence of ADD in a child within this category (classic). Their behavior, at home or school, is the primary piece of information that a professional uses to diagnose the classic ADD child.

Before this book, children (or teens and adults) who did not exhibit the classic symptoms of ADD, were often overlooked or misdiagnosed.

This is the exact reason for this book.

The symptoms of ADD vary from age group to age group. They also vary within each age group. The symptoms are also affected by the ADD person's personal experiences, and individual personality.

Because of the aforementioned influences on an ADD person, it's obvious that all ADD people are not the same.

All ADD people have the exact basic problems, but each ADD person does not manifest these problems in the same way.

When I say manifest their problems differently, I simply mean that each person may have the same symptom, but to a different degree.

Example: The classic ADD child is easily distracted by sounds and movements. They respond to these distractions by constantly looking around, or getting up and investigating the distractions when they should be doing their school work.

On the other hand, the complex ADD child is also distracted by sounds and movements. However, they do not constantly look around or leave their chair. They can't concentrate on their work because of these distractions, but no one recognizes this because their behavior is not disruptive.

Other traits of the classic ADD child is that he is more violent and physical than other ADD children. He talks back to adults and may threaten them with physical harm.

The classic ADD child may pose problems for parents and teachers. He may steal and lie more often than other ADD children. He exhibits the characteristics commonly known as "hyperactive". This excessive activity started at an early age (perhaps while still in the womb). They were difficult for the parents to monitor. The classic ADD child needs very little sleep and doesn't take daily naps. Consequently, they are awake when the parents are asleep. Because of this, they wander out of their rooms or out of the house, sometimes in the middle of the night.

The classic ADD child is primarily a behavior problem but he also exhibits academic problems. They are impulsive and respond to their feelings of the moment. They don't consider the long term consequences of their actions.

Traditional testing methods are often adequate in determining the presence of ADD in the classic ADD child.

The ADD symptoms in this category are a combination of behavioral and academic problems.

The behavioral problems are not as severe as those in the classic ADD child. They also may not occur as often.

The symptoms of ADD are observable, but are not as blatant as those found in classic ADD. Therefore, it may be necessary to examine the child's academic performance as well as their behavior.

The traditional academic tests used by schools and professionals may be adequate in discovering the problems of the semi-classic ADD child.

Other techniques that may be adequate for the semi-classic ADD child include parent and teacher questionnaires. Achievement tests for reading, writing, math and phonics are also useful in determining the specific problems of the semi-classic ADD child.

The semi-classic ADD child may be a behavior problem at home but not at school. The reverse may also be true. This is one of the reasons that teachers and parents become "adversaries". In other words, one adult doesn't see what the other adult sees. Therefore, the adult who claims that the child is a behavior problem, is not believed. If they are believed, the adult may be seen as the "cause" of the child's misbehavior. In essence, the parent blames the teacher or the teacher blames the parent. This also occurs between parents who are divorced. The parent who lives with the child 90% of the time, is often blamed for the child's misbehavior. The parent who only visits the child a few weeks per year, may not see the child's behavior problems as clearly as the other parent.

Child Category III

(Semi-Complex)

The ADD symptoms of the Semi-Complex category are primarily <u>academic</u>.

Some of these academic problems are obvious to the casual observer and some are not.

Behavioral problems are <u>not</u> a major factor in the Semi-Complex category. This means that excessive activity may <u>not</u> exist in the semi-complex ADD child.

To the casual observer, the semi-complex ADD child may appear to be "normal." In other words, their outward appearance is <u>not</u> out of the ordinary and their academic grades are <u>not</u> extremely poor.

In order to discover the academic problems of the semi-complex child, a more comprehensive testing procedure must be utilized. The traditional tests used by the schools or professionals are <u>not</u> adequate. In fact, the semi-complex ADD child may perform well on these traditional tests. The reason for this is due to several factors. One factor is that the tests are only geared to measure <u>severe</u> academic problems. They are <u>not</u> geared to test for the subtle symptoms of the semi-complex ADD child.

Another factor that makes these tests ineffective is the <u>method</u> in which they are presented. By the term "<u>method</u>," I'm speaking of the <u>structure</u> of the testing environment. The environment is <u>controlled</u>, and the examiner encourages the child to perform as well as possible. The child is <u>alone</u> with <u>one</u> adult, in a <u>quiet</u> room. In other words, the problems that the ADD child encounters every day (ie: distractions by sounds and movements in the classroom), have been <u>eliminated</u>. Therefore, the semi-complex ADD child will be able to do well on any test with which he is presented. The results of these traditional tests will be misleading.

Another factor that makes traditional testing ineffective for the semi-complex ADD child is their level of intelligence. These ADD children often have above average intelligence. Consequently, they score well on these traditional tests. This will lead the examiner to false conclusions. They will see <u>no</u> signs of a problem and will disregard the possibility of this child having ADD.

Child Category IV

(Complex)

The name of this category (Complex) is self-explanatory.
Needless to say, the ADD symptoms of this category are not
directly observable.

The major problems the complex ADD child may exhibit are
emotional. They experience emotional problems, stress,
depression, and fear, because they must struggle to maintain
concentration and avoid distractions. The distractions the
complex ADD child encounters are often thoughts and ideas
that are not within their control (unless they are treated with
medication).

The effort they must put forth to avoid these intruding
thoughts can not be measured. They may not be able to
explain these intruding thoughts because they are "normal"
occurrences to them. They have nothing with which it can be
compared. They don't know that other people don't have
these intruding thoughts. Therefore, they may assume that
they just need to "try harder" to control them.

This is where frustration and disappointment may overwhelm
them.

If these intruding thoughts continue, they may misinterpret
this as a sign of their failure to control them. In other words,
they blame themselves. This self-blame is often reinforced by
the comments of adults. Adults often say, "You just need to
try a little harder."

These adults have good intentions when they make these comments. Unfortunately, they don't realize that the child is trying hard. In fact, they are trying harder than most children.

The misunderstanding revolves around the fact that neither person (adult or child) knows that the child has complex ADD. If this was known, both of them would understand that "trying harder" is futile.

ADD is a physical problem (chemical imbalance) and "trying harder" will not balance the chemical.

The complex ADD child is difficult to diagnose, even with comprehensive testing. The testing methods that are needed for this category require a specific approach. (My evaluation process is not included in this book. However, it is specifically geared to test the complex and semi-complex ADD children, teens, and adults.)

The traditional testing methods are absolutely ineffective with the complex ADD child. The reason for their ineffectiveness is due to the child's high intelligence level, personality traits, and conscientious parents (and other possible reasons).

The parents may play a part in the ADD child's ability to perform adequately. They may have hired tutors or sent the child to learning centers or private schools. They may have worked with the child every night for 3 or 4 hours in order to keep the child from making poor grades. The child may do a great deal of extra work near the end of the grading period in order to inflate their grades.

In order to recognize the complex ADD child, it is necessary to do more than look for ADD symptoms. It is necessary to look for <u>signs</u> that ADD symptoms <u>exist</u>. However, don't expect them to be as obvious as the symptoms of the classic ADD child.

In this category, you must examine <u>other</u> information that is <u>not</u> <u>directly</u> related to ADD.

Here is the best way to approach this category:

1. Remember that the person with whom you are dealing, has a problem of some kind, or you wouldn't be investigating the possibility of their having ADD.

2. Look for <u>subtle</u> signs of ADD. In other words, look for the same ADD symptoms that are listed in the other ADD categories, but don't expect them to be as obvious or occur as often.

3. Look for possible explanations as to <u>why</u> their ADD symptoms are not as blatant as those of the classic or semi-classic ADD child. (ie: intelligence, personality, parents, etc.)

4. Try to <u>rule</u> <u>out</u> ADD as an explanation. In other words, try to find other possible reasons for this child's problems. This child is receiving your attention for "some" reason. Therefore, someone feels that <u>some</u> <u>kind</u> of problem exists.

   Things to ask yourself: Did the child recently have a devastating experience; Have they recently moved; Has he had an accident; etc., etc.

5. Compare ADD with the other possible explanations for this child's problems. Which one seems more reasonable? Did you have to combine <u>several</u> possible alternative explanations in order to account for <u>all</u> the problems they experience? Be wary of this, because other possible explanations <u>always</u> exist. Therefore, you must use common sense in coming to a final conclusion, especially if you <u>rule</u> <u>out</u> ADD.

Always remember the following:

a. ADD is <u>much</u> more common than other disorders.

b. This child is thought to have <u>some</u> kind of problem. Therefore, <u>listen</u> to what those close to the child report. (Read between the lines). Listen to the <u>parents</u>. They know their child better than anyone.

c. "Bad" parents do <u>not</u> seek help for their child. Therefore, <u>don't</u> jump to conclusions about the parents. <u>They</u> are the ones who took the initiative to find help for their child.

d. If other alternative explanations for the child's problems are presented, are they <u>complex</u> and <u>theoretical</u>? In other words, do these other explanations rely on "unclear" psychological theories that are difficult to prove? Beware of "over-psychologizing."

e. Before blaming the parents, consider their
other children. If the other children
have no problems, how do you explain
this?

f. Individual differences. This statement is
illogical, if you blame the parents. In
fact, it rules out the parents.
"Individual differences" points out the
fact that this individual is different
from other siblings or children. This is
correct. This difference is what you are
looking for. What is this individual
difference?

g. Ask about other family members. ADD
is hereditary. Therefore, investigate
the possibility of ADD in other family
members (biological family). This
includes aunts, uncles, grandparents,
etc.

h. Don't be afraid to say; "I don't know."
If you are unclear as to whether or not
this child has complex ADD, admit it.
This is better than making a definite
statement that they don't have ADD.
It may be necessary to wait for a year
or more before a definite answer can
be given (yes or no).

i. If your final conclusion is that you don't
know, the next decision is for the
parents.

If, after <u>thorough</u> <u>testing</u> for ADD, no clear decision can be made, the <u>treatment</u> for ADD may have to be used as the <u>final</u> test. I dislike this approach, but if the parents want to try the medication for 1 or 2 <u>weeks</u> to see if it helps the child, then it's their decision.

I developed an evaluation process in order to <u>avoid</u> the use of medication as a <u>testing</u> method. In years past, this is how medication received a bad reputation. Since there was no testing process for ADD, professionals used the treatment (medication) as <u>the</u> <u>test</u>. In other words, the <u>treatment</u> was given <u>to</u> <u>determine</u> the diagnosis of ADD. If the medication helped, then the child had ADD. If it didn't help, then they didn't have ADD. This is exactly the opposite of how things should be done. This is why I developed an evaluation process for ADD. <u>My</u> <u>testing</u> <u>is</u> <u>always</u> done <u>before</u> a diagnosis is made. A <u>diagnosis</u> <u>is</u> <u>made</u> <u>before</u> the treatment is implemented (ie: medication).

Unfortunately, there is a <u>very</u> <u>small</u> <u>percentage</u> of ADD people who can't be detected by <u>any</u> evaluation process.

Teen
Categories

Teen Category I

(Classic)

<u>All</u> of the Teen Categories rely upon the results from the Child Categories.

The reason for this, is because the age difference between the child and teen consists of only a few years. A child and teen are still in similar situations. Both are in school and live with their parents (or they are under the guidance of some adult).

Because of the similarities, the results of the Child Categories will still be relevant for a teenager. In other words, if a teenager had ADD as a child, it's unlikely that these traits have disappeared in only 2 or 3 years. Therefore, close attention should be paid to the results of the Child Categories.

In essence, the teen categories are needed to provide a consistent view of an ADD person from childhood to adulthood. This is why the information in the ADD Teen Categories is not as comprehensive as the Child and Adult Categories.

Of all the teen categories, the classic ADD teens are the easiest to recognize.

Most of them were classic ADD children. The only things that have changed, are their interests. Once again, behavior is the major problem of the classic ADD teen.

In order to classify an ADD teen as classic, the first thing that should be done, is to consider the child categories. In other words, there should be a <u>history</u> of ADD that was obvious even as a child. The reason for this is because ADD is hereditary, and is present from birth. ADD doesn't occur overnight.

Some classic ADD teens may <u>not</u> have been classic ADD children. Therefore, all of the child categories should be investigated.

The difficulty in diagnosing <u>any</u> ADD teen is related to their age. Other problems may have developed over the years. These other problems are often <u>easier</u> to see than ADD. Therefore, it is easy to overlook ADD.

These other problems become the focus of parents or professionals. This is especially true if this teen was <u>never</u> diagnosed as having ADD as a child. It is falsely assumed that, if a teen had ADD, this would have been discovered earlier. This is not the case. Many ADD children are overlooked as having ADD. Consequently, they are also overlooked as having ADD as teenagers.

Traits of the classic ADD teen include dropping out of school, alcohol/drug abuse, disruptive behavior, and skipping school. They may be under the supervision of the Juvenile Probation Department because of their behavior problems at home or school. Some may be sent to facilities for 24-hour care.

Again, the classic ADD teen has more behavior problems than the other ADD teen categories.

Teen Category II

(Semi-Classic)

The Semi-Classic ADD Teen category involves behavior and academic problems. As stated earlier, they also had ADD as a child, regardless of whether or not they had been diagnosed.

Once again, it's necessary to investigate the child categories before making a decision about the ADD teen. If they have ADD as a teen, then they had it as a child.

Semi-classic ADD teens may have behavior problems but not to the degree of the classic ADD teen. The same is true of academic problems. They may exhibit problems (behavior or academic) at intervals. They may do well for a month or two and then do poorly. There are a number of reasons for this. All of the possible reasons can't be listed, but the basic reason is due to their inability to consistently "compensate" for the symptoms of ADD. Because they are teenagers, they must cope with more than ADD. This means that they have more to cope with than teenagers who don't have ADD. This is stressful.

The semi-classic ADD teen may be considered a "nerd" or immature instead of mean and rambunctious.

They may be "at risk" of dropping out of school or becoming involved in drugs or alcohol. They can be easily influenced or manipulated by peers because of their comprehension problems. They may be unable to decipher the motivation of others or anticipate the possible consequences of certain behaviors.

The behavior problems these teens may cause in the classroom are due to clowning around or acting silly. They are prone to being followers. Therefore, the type of people with whom they associate will have a strong influence on the "direction" they take.

<u>Testing</u>:

Traditional testing may be adequate in diagnosing the semi-classic teen.

Teen Category III

(Semi-Complex)

The primary problems of the semi-complex ADD teen revolves around academic work. Their behavior or emotional status is <u>not</u> the main feature or trait of this category. However, their behavior and emotional well-being is often affected by the frustration and stress they endure because of their academic problems.

The semi-complex ADD teen is extremely intelligent but his grades may not reflect this. They may be misdiagnosed as having a disability such as an "auditory processing" problem or "dyslexia". They may actually have symptoms that resemble these "learning disabilities", but their having semi-complex ADD may be the reason for these symptoms. In some instances, they may have these other learning problems <u>and</u> semi-complex ADD. However, semi-complex ADD is the most important problem because it will make these other problems more difficult to overcome.

In other words, the symptoms of ADD will "<u>intensify</u>" other learning problems and cause them to be <u>more</u> <u>severe</u>.

This is why the semi-complex ADD teen is often overlooked. These other "learning problems" are more easily identified as a problem and professionals often stop looking for other possible problems such as ADD. Ironically, when a "learning disability" is recognized, this should immediately alert the professional to the possibility of ADD. This is due to the fact that research clearly shows that ADD is <u>more</u> common than these other learning problems and often <u>causes</u> these problems.

27

If the semi-complex ADD teen was diagnosed as having a "learning disability" as a child (and not ADD), this increases the chances that ADD will not be investigated as a possible problem.

This is why the ADD Child categories must be examined before the Teen and Adult categories. In essence, you must consider the possibility that this teen was overlooked or misdiagnosed as a child.

Traditional testing may detect some of the problems of the semi-complex ADD teen but a more comprehensive test is also needed. Also, as stated earlier, an examination of the Child categories is helpful in identifying any ADD teen or adult.

Teen Category IV

(Complex)

Of all the teen categories, the complex ADD teen is the most difficult to diagnose.

As stated throughout this book, the older an ADD person becomes, the more life experiences they have. These other life experiences can result in problems that are not due to ADD. Therefore, it is sometimes difficult to separate the problems caused by ADD from those caused by these other life experiences.

It is easy to overlook the complex ADD teen because of these other life experiences. This is because the symptoms of complex ADD are not as easily identified as are other life experiences. For example: If a complex ADD teen lost a parent, this event may be seen as the only reason for the teen's behavior or poor academic performance. In other words, ADD will not be investigated as a possible problem because the loss of a parent is much more obvious and seems to be a logical explanation for the teen's problems. In fact, this may be the case, but this doesn't necessarily rule out complex ADD. We must remember that it is possible to have more than one problem at a time. Unfortunately, many complex ADD teens are overlooked because professionals jump to conclusions instead of investigating further.

This is why the child categories must be investigated before the teen or adult ADD categories. If a teen has complex ADD, then they have always had ADD. ADD is a physical problem (chemical imbalance) and the signs of ADD were present when they were children. Another life experience (such as the death of a parent) may affect the complex ADD teen but it is not the <u>cause</u> of their ADD. This other life experience may be the "straw that broke the camel's back."

In other words, the complex ADD teen has always had to struggle harder to cope with life than non-ADD teens. Consequently, when another negative life experience (losing a parent) is introduced into their life, they may no longer be able to cope as well as they did before this event. In essence, their coping ability has reached its limit.

The complex ADD teen is unlike the complex ADD child or complex ADD adult. The complex ADD teen may have severe behavior problems or they may be an overachiever who does well in school. The reason for this wide variation is primarily due to their age. The teen years are the most difficult for anyone, regardless of ADD. The most important factors in determining how the complex ADD teen develops, are the experiences he encounters during these years, and how he copes with them. This will vary from person to person. Therefore, there will be some complex ADD teens who cope well and others who will not.

The traditional testing procedures will <u>not</u> be effective for the complex ADD teen. A more comprehensive testing procedure must be utilized. The tests should specifically target the symptoms of ADD. Also, the results from the child categories will be extremely important in diagnosing the complex ADD teen.

Adult
Categories

Adult Category I

(Classic)

Of all the adult categories, this is the most easily identified and described. However, all ADD adults are more difficult to recognize than children or teens. This is due to the fact that adults have had more life experiences.

These other experiences could result in problems that are <u>not</u> due to ADD. This is why you must begin with the child categories, even when ADD is suspected in an adult. If an adult has ADD, they have had it since childhood. There is no definite pattern as to which child category the adult may have had as a child. In other words, the classic ADD adult was not necessarily a classic ADD child or teen. Therefore, all of the child and teen categories must be examined before examining the adult categories.

In this category, Classic ADD Adult, severe behavior problems are the predominant traits. There is a high probability that this classic ADD adult was a classic ADD teen. This may depend on their current age. For example: If they were a classic ADD teen at 16, and they are now only 19, there is a good chance that some of the classic ADD teen traits remain unchanged.

On the other hand, if they were a complex ADD teen at age 16, and they are now 35, they may have deteriorated over these 19 years to the point that they are now a classic ADD adult.

To repeat the point made earlier: Do not assume that the classic ADD Adult was a classic ADD teen or child. Age and circumstances can affect how the ADD adult develops.

The classic ADD adult will exhibit severe problems such as alcohol, drug abuse, criminal behavior, violence toward a spouse or others.

They may be in prison or on parole. They may have a very bad and quick temper, but can be very charming and manipulative.

They are often energetic and have a high tolerance for pain. This allows them to be active or awake for 16 or 18 hours per day. They often work very hard for a short period of time, but are unable to be consistent and stick with a job.

Because they are manipulative and charming, they can impress a potential employer but after they are hired, their productivity declines. Consequently, they have had many jobs that only lasted a short period of time.

They are irresponsible with money, and may be deeply in debt.

The classic ADD adult may have the same traits of the other Adult categories, but the classic ADD adult has more severe behavior problems.

Testing:

Traditional testing will not be effective in determining the presence of ADD in the classic ADD adult. This is primarily due to their age. Even if they have academic problems, they are able to perform adequately on a test that only lasts a short time. Therefore, the results will not be accurate.

A review of their academic records will reveal more than traditional tests. If they were tested as a child, these results could be helpful. If report cards are available, these are valuable in determining their performance both academically and behaviorally. The comment section on report cards can also give an insight into how the teacher evaluated their performance. Look for key words or phrases such as: needs to pay attention, doesn't turn in his work, disrupts class. Note if these are mentioned often by different teachers or at different grade levels.

Traditional testing may indicate some continued academic problems that are present in the classic ADD adult. If academic problems are evident, this indicates <u>severe</u> problems. It is uncommon to find a classic ADD adult that has such severe problems, but some do have such problems.

For all adults, a personality test can be helpful. Personality traits of ADD adults are rather similar, regardless of their success or job. Impulsiveness and lack of attention to detail, are two traits that may show up on their personality tests. There are several, so don't expect every ADD adult to have the exact same personality traits. Everyone is different, even ADD adults.

Adult Category II

(Semi-Classic)

Because most adults are no longer involved in school, the semi-classic ADD adult is not as easily described as the semi-classic ADD child. There are no clearly observable distinctions between behavior and academic problems of the semi-classic ADD adult. This is why the results from the child and teen categories are important when diagnosing any ADD adult.

The semi-classic ADD adult is apt to be on the "borderline" of being a drug or alcohol abuser. They may function adequately in a work situation, but not advance to upper management. They may have problems in a marital relationship, but can maintain the relationship longer than the classic ADD adult. Their relationships may be "unsteady", but they are able to maintain them.

Traditional testing will not be adequate for identifying the semi-classic ADD adult. As stated earlier, all ADD adults often do well on the traditional tests due to their age and experience. Personality testing is highly recommended for the semi-classic ADD adult because the traits of ADD are often clearly evident (ie: impulsiveness, distractibility, etc.). Therefore, using the personality testing along with the information from the child and teen categories may be adequate in identifying the semi-classic ADD adult.

Adult Category III

(Semi-Complex)

This category is similar to the Complex ADD adult. There is no big distinct difference between the two. The main difference between the two is that some of the symptoms of the semi-complex ADD adult may be observable to others.

The specific symptoms that may be observable cannot be predicted because each person is different. Some may have academic problems that are observable and others may have some emotional problems that are observable.

Again, the child and teen categories must be examined before the adult categories. Those categories will provide a great deal of information. The results of the child and teen categories will increase or decrease the probability that this adult has ADD.

The traditional testing used by professionals will <u>not</u> be effective with the semi-complex ADD adult. A personality test can be very helpful.

The semi-complex adult is likely to have observable problems that have been <u>caused</u> by the <u>symptoms</u> <u>of</u> <u>ADD</u>. However, these problems have often been diagnosed as something other than ADD. The ADD is "masked" by these other observable problems. In other words, the semi-complex ADD adult may be diagnosed as "depressed" instead of ADD. The diagnosis of "<u>depression</u>" is often <u>correct,</u> but the cause of the depression goes <u>undetected</u>.

This is why the semi-complex and complex ADD adult is hard to diagnose. Their ADD has resulted in emotional problems such as depression. Professionals often diagnose what they observe without considering ADD.

The semi-complex ADD adult may have been diagnosed as having other "psychological" or "emotional" problems. It's important to take note of this when gathering the information. Depression is the most common "misdiagnosis" but it's not the only one. Therefore, don't assume that their previous psychological or emotional problems are necessarily "correct". In other words, don't rule out semi-complex ADD until you have compiled as much information as possible.

Adult Category IV

(Complex)

Of all 12 ADD categories, this one is the most difficult to characterize. Consequently, it's the most difficult to diagnose.

The first reason for its complexity is similar to that of the other adult categories; you are dealing with adults. Their life experiences may have complicated the "picture". These other experiences may have caused problems that are not due to ADD. Therefore, it will be difficult to separate the ADD from these other experiences.

The specific traits of the complex ADD adult are not as clearly identified as they are in the other categories. Because of this, a unique approach to diagnosing them must be utilized. You not only look for symptoms of ADD, you must look for reasons for the symptoms to be masked or not easily identified.

In other words, you must be biased in your approach to the complex ADD adult. By the word biased, I only mean that you must gather information about this adult, under the assumption that they have ADD.

Remember, you are only biased when gathering the information. When all of the information has been gathered, you no longer use this biased approach. When it's time to make a decision, you must be objective in your examination of all available information. You must look for other possible explanations.

41

The most important information is the results of this adult's child and teen categories. The child and teen categories may reveal the existence of ADD at an early age. If the symptoms existed at an early age, this is just as important as the information gathered on the adult's <u>current</u> life.

The complex ADD adult is extremely intelligent and intuitive. Therefore, they can compensate for the problems that their ADD causes. Those around them are unaware of their problems. The only people who may recognize a problem, are those adults who live with them every day. The complex ADD adult may recognize they have a problem, but rarely mention this to others. They just continue to compensate for these problems because they don't see themselves as having a problem. They may interpret their struggles as an ordinary part of life. They assume that <u>everyone</u> faces these struggles.

In essence, they are correct. <u>Everyone</u> struggles with the same problems in life. However, the difference between the ADD person and others, is the <u>degree</u> of <u>effort</u> <u>and</u> <u>time</u> that the ADD person must use in order to overcome these struggles.

Here is the best way to approach this category:

1. Remember that the person with whom you are dealing, has a problem of some kind, or you wouldn't be investigating the possibility of their having ADD.

2. Look for <u>subtle</u> signs of ADD. In other words, look for the same ADD symptoms that are listed in other ADD categories, but don't expect them to be as obvious or occur as often.

3. Look for possible explanations as to <u>why</u> their ADD symptoms are not as blatant as those of the other categories (ie: intelligence, personality, etc.).

4. Try to <u>rule out</u> ADD as an explanation. In other words, try to find other possible reasons for this adult's problems. This adult is receiving your attention for "some" reason. Therefore, someone feels that <u>some kind</u> of problem exists.

   Ask yourself: what other life experiences could be the cause of this person's problems?

5. Compare ADD with the other possible explanations for this person's problems. Which one seems more reasonable? Did you have to combine several possible alternative explanations in order to account for all the problems they experience? Be wary of this, because other possible explanations always exist. Therefore, you must use common sense in coming to a final conclusion, especially if you rule out ADD.

   Things to use common sense about:

   a. Always remember; ADD is <u>much</u> more common than other disorders.

   b. This person is thought to have <u>some</u> kind of problem. Therefore, <u>listen</u> to what those close to them report. (Read between the lines).

c. If other alternative explanations for these problems are presented, are they complex and theoretical? In other words, do these other explanations rely on "unclear" psychological theories that are difficult to prove? Beware of "over-psychologizing."

d. Ask about other family members. ADD is hereditary. Therefore, investigate the possibility of ADD in other family members (biological family). This includes aunts, uncles, grandparents, etc.

e. Don't be afraid to say; "I don't know." If you are unclear as to whether or not this person has complex ADD, admit it. This is better than making a definite statement that they don't have ADD. It may be necessary to wait for a year or more before a definite answer can be given (yes or no).

f. If your final conclusion is that you don't know, the next decision is for the person.

If, after thorough testing for ADD, no clear decision can be made, the treatment for ADD may have to be used as the final test. I dislike this approach, but if they want to try the medication for 1 or 2 weeks to see if it helps, then it's their decision. Obviously, the doctor will also have to agree to prescribe it.

As stated earlier, I developed an evaluation process in order to <u>avoid</u> the use of medication as a <u>testing</u> method. In years past, this is how medication received a bad reputation. Since there was no testing process for ADD, professionals used the treatment (medication) as <u>the</u> <u>test</u>. In other words, the <u>treatment</u> was given <u>to</u> <u>determine</u> the diagnosis of ADD. If the medication helped, then the child had ADD. If it didn't help, then they didn't have ADD. This is exactly the opposite of how things should be done. This is why I developed an evaluation process for ADD. <u>My</u> <u>testing</u> <u>is</u> <u>always</u> done <u>before</u> a diagnosis is made. A <u>diagnosis</u> <u>is</u> <u>made</u> <u>before</u> the treatment is implemented (ie: medication).

Unfortunately, there is a <u>very</u> <u>small</u> <u>percentage</u> of ADD people who can't be detected by <u>any</u> evaluation process. Therefore, this method is the only alternative, other than <u>not</u> trying at all.

SECTION B

Checklists

Directions

1. This section is separated into 3 parts:

    a. Child Categories (Ages 2 to 13)

    b. Teen Categories (Ages 13 to 19)

    c. Adult Categories (Ages 17 and above)

2. Start with the child categories (regardless of the person's age).

3. There is an "overlap" in the teen and adult categories. The teen categories include the ages 17, 18, and 19 because of the academic information that may be pertinent to this person.

4. If the person is an Adult, it will still be necessary to examine the child and teen categories.

5. You must use common sense when using these categories. Sometimes, there is not a clear distinction as to which category an ADD person belongs. Therefore, make note of the items that describe them, even if they are located in a different category.

6. Remember: you are trying to determine if this person has ADD. The specific category is not that important. These categories are merely a way to reduce the confusion as to why a person doesn't have every symptom or trait of ADD.

PART ONE

Child
Categories

(Through Age 12)

Child

Category I

(Classic)

Child Category I

(Classic)

Section A

* <u>Diagnosed</u> as having a learning disability (ie: Dyslexia, comprehension problems, auditory processing problems).

* Extremely active physically (most of the time, not just occasionally).

* <u>Extremely</u> bad temper (hits other children in a violent manner or hits back at adults when angry).

* Abnormal EEG patterns.

If <u>none</u> of the above are checked, stop here and proceed to Category II. The child does <u>not</u> meet the criteria for Category I.

If one or more of the above are checked, continue with Section B of this category.

Section B

* Gets up in the middle of the night and roams the house or goes outside without parents' awareness.

* Steals from stores, parents, or other children <u>often</u>.

* Talks of suicide, death, or killing someone (or has actually killed an animal such as a cat or dog).

* Other family members are alcohol/drug abusers.

If <u>none</u> of the above are checked, stop here and proceed to Category II. The child does <u>not</u> meet the criteria for Category I.

If one or more of the above are checked, continue with Section C of this category.

Section C

* Curses parents and other adults.

* Openly refuses to obey adults (They don't just say no and then comply. They continue to resist until the incident escalates into a "War of Wills").

* Lies often, even over little things that are unimportant (They "make up" extraordinary stories that are convincing because of the elaborate details they give).

* They may yell, scream, clench teeth, run around, or jump for no apparent reason. It's as if they just "had" to release some pent-up energy.

* They need very little sleep (They may be unable to take naps in the middle of the day).

If none of the above are checked, stop here and proceed to Category II. The child does not meet the criteria for Category I.

If one or more of the above are checked, continue with Section D of this category.

Section D

* Accident prone (Has lots of bumps or bruises because they are careless).

* Plays with fire <u>often</u>.

* Very disorganized.

* High pain tolerance (Note: This is demonstrated when they <u>don't</u> <u>know</u> that what they experienced is <u>supposed</u> to hurt. They may cry only after an adult reacts).

* Bed-wetter (beyond the expected accidents of a child their age).

* Left-Handed (or ambidextrous).

If <u>none</u> of the above are checked, stop here and proceed to Category II. The child does <u>not</u> meet the criteria for Category I.

If one or more of the above are checked, continue with Section E of this category.

Section E

* Disrupts class often.

* Plays rough with other children.

* Over-reacts emotionally (this applies to anger as well as excitement).

* Hard for them to sit for a long period of time, especially during meals (This does not include playing or watching television. They may be able to do these for hours).

* Forgets or loses things often.

If none of the above are checked, stop here and proceed to Category II. The child does not meet the criteria for Category I.

If one or more of the above are checked, continue with Section F of this category.

Section F

* Easily distracted (visually and auditorily).

* Has more trouble learning to tie their shoes than others their age.

* Adopted (one or more parent unknown or they were adopted through an agency. Don't mark this if adoption is only due to a step-parent).

* Needs more attention than others to get them to complete homework or tasks.

Child

Category II

(Semi-Classic)

Child Category II

(Semi-Classic)

Section A

* Diagnosed as learning disabled (Dyslexia, etc.).

* Quiet, shy or withdrawn.

* Extremely sensitive (feelings hurt easily).

* Abnormal EEG.

* Impulsive in <u>behaviors</u> (Not in a "mean" way. Does things without thinking of the consequences).

* Daydreams <u>often</u>.

* Takes an excessive amount of time to complete tasks or to do homework.

* Has to be given instructions one at a time, or reminded several times in order to get them to comply.

* Other family members have been diagnosed as having ADD.

If <u>none</u> of the above are checked, stop here and proceed to Category III. The child does <u>not</u> meet the criteria for Category II.

If one or more of the above are checked, continue with Section B of this category.

Section B

* Often fails to complete homework; or, completes it but doesn't turn it in.

* Impulsive in school <u>work</u> (ie: makes simple careless mistakes that have <u>nothing</u> <u>to</u> <u>do</u> with their knowledge).

* Often forgets what they are told.

* Is a behavior problem at home but not at school.

If <u>none</u> of the above are checked, stop here and proceed to Category III. The child does <u>not</u> meet the criteria for Category II.

If one or more of the above are checked, continue with Section C of this category.

Child Category II

Section C

*   Easily distracted by sounds.

*   Behavior problems at school but not at home.

*   Loses things often (ie: shoes, jackets, school papers).

*   Over-reacts emotionally (This includes anger, depression, and excitement).

*   Doesn't ask questions in the classroom even if they don't understand the directives.

*   Can play video games for long periods but can't sit and concentrate on school work without being prompted.

Child

Category III

(Semi-Complex)

Child Category III

(Semi-Complex)

----

*   Poor reader.

*   Poor speller.

*   Poor handwriting.

*   They prefer to print, even though they are able to write cursive.

*   They interpret things "rigidly" (ie: They seem to lack common sense).

*   Report card grades are low due to a large number of 0's for work not turned in.

*   They overlook or skip problems (especially in math) for no obvious reason.

*   Disorganized in their approach to school work (You must observe them to discover this. They may jump from items at the top of the page to items at the bottom; or, they go from left to right and then right to left).

*   Their grades are not up to their abilities (Their grades may be passing but they aren't performing as well as would be expected when their intelligence level is considered. Or, they seem to have to work harder than they should).

* They become frustrated with their school work (Compared to other children or siblings, they appear to be more frustrated).

* When reading aloud, they often stop and re-read the sentence because they either omitted or inserted a word.

* Their handwriting can be good when they slow down and take their time. However, they must go very slow or, their writing becomes very small or very large.

* They fluctuate from printing to cursive within the same sentence, paragraph, or word.

* When they copy from the board, or book, they leave out information or copy the wrong words or numbers.

* If there are 2 parts of written instructions, they do one (usually the first one) and overlook, or forget, the other.

* Is a behavior problem because of clowning around and immature behavior. They are not mean or violent.

* They have trouble combining information and understanding how it fits together. They may understand each individual piece of information, but not how the pieces fit together.

* They make simple careless mistakes in schoolwork, especially in math. They may correctly answer difficult problems, but miss some of the simple ones.

Child Category III
---

*   Their report card grades widely fluctuate each grading period (ie: 3A's - 2F's one period and then reverses to 3F's - 2A's on the next).

*   Teachers report no major problems but often comments that he needs to "try harder".

*   They become overwhelmed when presented with a full page of school work (such as math).

*   They mis-read words, even though they may correct it later (ie: They may say "this" instead of "the").

*   The night before a spelling test, they correctly spell the words. However, on the day of the test, they misspell several.

*   In math, their ability fluctuates from problem to problem (Example: Item #4 may be similar to item #9. After an adult explains how to do #4, they understand. However, when they reach item #9, they appear to be unable to see the connection to item #4. They seem to have "forgotten").

*   "Appears" to be Dyslexic at times because they pronounce "saw" as "was" (or other words with similar letters). However, when these words are isolated and presented alone, they pronounce them properly.

*   They hold their pencil in an unusual fashion.

71

* They have problems separating the important from the unimportant (ie: They remember the trivial aspects of a reading assignment but overlook the major concept or thought).

Child

Category IV

(Complex)

* Extremely intelligent but their grades are not as high as would be expected.

* Good grades, but the amount of effort and time expended is excessive.

* Has a pleasant personality, is well liked, and therefore receives extra help from teachers or receives "inflated" grades (unofficially).

* Does a lot of "extra" work just before report card time, in order to bring up their grades.

* They receive tutoring or other individualized help to keep good grades.

* The parents go to extraordinary effort to make sure the child gets good grades (more than the average child receives).

* The child is extremely self-motivated and constantly pushes himself to make good grades (more effort than they should with their high intelligence).

* Attended a private school for the small classes and more individualized attention.

* Occasionally cheats, but no one says anything because he's smart, well liked, and puts out a great deal of effort most of the time.

* Has received home schooling for one-on-one help.

* Their high grades in one area (ie: tests) bring up their very low grades in another (ie: homework).

* Numerous report card comments such as; Needs to put forth more effort; Needs to pay attention; Doesn't complete assignments.

* Good grades in regular classes but only <u>average</u> or borderline grades in the <u>advanced</u> classes.

* Overly organized to the point of appearing to be obsessive/compulsive (They crave organization and dislike changes).

* They express themselves well and openly complain of not being able to concentrate, remember things, or of being distracted by sounds.

* They have <u>no</u> allergies or unusual eating habits.

* Their grades fluctuate every grading period (ie: 3 classes are high, 3 are low. Next grading period, these are opposite).

*   They seem to have stomach problems or headaches during the school year but few during vacation or non-school days (Sunday nights may be when they start).

*   Their problems, emotional or behavioral, seem to coincide with the school year but not on vacations.

*   Made very good grades until they reached the 4th grade; or when they started a grade that required them to change rooms every hour or so.

*   They seem to have quit putting forth as much effort as they once did.

*   They are more critical of themselves for their inability to achieve than the parents or teachers.

*   Occasionally, they may shock adults with a comment about wanting to be dead or not deserving to live.

*   Overly sensitive to the feelings of others (May even show concern for the financial status of their parents by wanting to help them save money).

*   They don't want to burden their parents with their frustration with school so they may become depressed and not explain why.

*   Parents or another adult suggests that the child needs counseling because of a suspected emotional problem.

Child Category IV

* An emotional problem is suspected as the cause of their "sub-par" academic performance or depression.

* Other family members (biological) have been diagnosed as having ADD or learning disabilities. This includes cousins, uncles, aunts, etc.

* There are several family members (biological) that are alcoholic or drug abusers. This includes cousins, aunts, uncles, etc.

* Other family members have been involved in illegal activities (regardless of whether or not they have been caught or convicted).

* Has been diagnosed as school phobic or separation anxiety disorder (These are more severe than just not wanting to go to school or leave their parents).

* Their emotional well-being appears to be a bigger problem than their academic performance because their grades are adequate.

* The parents are extremely successful and they are seen as putting too much pressure on the child to succeed (Note: Other children in the family seem to be well adjusted and perform well; especially females).

* Formal testing shows average or above average abilities.

Child Category IV
----

*   Although formal testing shows <u>overall</u> above average
    abilities, there are a few areas that are <u>extremely below</u>
    their overall ability (Note: Their lowest scores may be
    higher than that of <u>other</u> children, but still below their
    own overall ability).

PART TWO

Teen
Categories

(Ages 13 to 19)

Teen

Category I

(Classic)

Teen Category I

(Classic)

Section A

* <u>Must</u> meet the criteria for one of the child categories. Therefore, you must start with Part One of this book.

* Diagnosed as having a learning disability.

* Extremely active physically.

* Abnormal EEG.

* Involved in alcohol/drug <u>abuse</u>.

* Involved in criminal activities.

* Violent (fights a lot).

* Dropped out of school.

* Has attempted suicide.

* Very bad grades.

If <u>none</u> of the above are checked, stop here and proceed to Category II. The teenager does <u>not</u> meet the criteria for Category I.

If one or more of the above are checked, continue with Section B of this category.

Section B

* Skips school often.

* Involved in gangs.

* Runs away from home or sneaks out often.

* Threatens parents or teachers with violence.

* Curses parents or other adults.

If none of the above are checked, stop here and proceed to Category II. The teenager does not meet the criteria for Category I.

If one or more of the above are checked, continue with Section C of this category.

Section C

* Sexually active or seems to be <u>overly</u> obsessed with sex.

* Picks friends who are similar (what parents would call "bad" friends).

* Insensitive to the feelings of others, but <u>overly</u> sensitive to their own feelings. They feel as if others treat them unfairly.

* Unrealistic goals or ideas (ie: They're going to get rich or be movie stars but have no concrete plans to work towards that goal. It's as if they are depending on <u>luck</u>).

Teen

Category II

(Semi-Classic)

Teen Category II

(Semi-Classic)

Section A

*   Diagnosed as having a learning disability (or called Dyslexic).

*   Met the criteria of one of the child categories.

*   Not excessively active. Almost the opposite (ie: depressed, withdrawn).

*   Very immature.

*   Is seen as an "at risk" student (ie: prone to drop out of school or become involved in alcohol/drugs).

*   Very low grades.

If none of the above are checked, stop here and proceed to Category III. The teenager does not meet the criteria for Category II.

If one or more of the above are checked, continue with Section B of this category.

Section B

* Numerous car accidents.

* Numerous traffic tickets.

* Sent to the principal's office more often than peers for clowning around or disruptive behavior.

* Associates with other teens who are "Trouble Makers".

* Experiments with alcohol or drugs more often than peers.

* History of allergies.

* EEG or brain wave abnormalities were found.

* Takes a lot of "risks" but doesn't necessarily do it on purpose. They don't realize the chance or risk they're taking.

* Very immature in many areas but shows advancement in others.

If <u>none</u> of the above are checked, stop here and proceed to Category III. The teenager does <u>not</u> meet the criteria for Category II.

If one or more of the above are checked, continue with Section C of this category.

Section C

*   The decisions they make don't seem to be well thought out (This is often why they get in trouble).

*   Gullible and easily manipulated by other teens who take advantage of them (even though he may feel smarter than others).

*   Dresses in an unusual fashion.

*   He feels picked on because he receives more discipline from teachers and parents than his siblings or peers.

*   Prone to blame others because they don't see how their behavior or decision contributed to their current predicament.

*   Highly verbal, but unable to carry on a conversation in which they must listen and follow the topic (ie: They have to control the conversation because they have trouble following one).

*   Very low grades.

Teen

Category III

(Semi-Complex)

Teen Category III

(Semi-Complex)

* Met the criteria for one of the child categories.

* Report card grades fluctuate each grading period.

* Grades are low, primarily because of 0's for not turning in work.

* Even if he can't catch on, he keeps coming back for help.

* Understands things better if he is read to, and doesn't have to read it himself.

* Directions have to be repeated often or he will forget.

* Directions have to be given one at a time.

* Interprets things rigidly or literally (ie: Doesn't seem to have common sense).

* Leaves out words or changes the order of numbers when copying from the board or a book.

* Handwriting can be very neat, but they must take their time and go very slow. Most of the time, it's very sloppy.

* They prefer printing and sometimes combine cursive and printing in the same word or sentence.

* Problems with fine motor skills (Example: They print because it's easier to control the pen to make short strokes. Cursive requires much more control because of the continuous "flow" across the page).

* They overlook or skip problems for no obvious reason.

* They have a disorganized approach to their work (ie: They jump around on the page for no obvious reason except to change the routine).

* Poor reader, especially if required to do so <u>aloud</u>. Has to read slowly.

* Not necessarily a poor reader, but when reading aloud, it is evident that they are unable to read as smoothly as others (ie: They have to re-start sentences; they leave out or insert words and pronounce words phonetically).

Teen

Category IV

(Complex)

Teen Category IV

(Complex)

---

* Met the criteria for one of the child categories.

* Is in advanced classes but doesn't do as well as one would expect.

* Makes good grades in regular classes but only average or below average in advanced classes.

* The amount of time and effort they put forth is excessive when their intelligence and ability is taken into account. Especially if their grades are only average or below.

* Is disorganized, but tries to be overly organized in some areas (ie: Has a container for pens, pencils, or a compartment for every feasible subject or class).

* Has a rigid routine for some areas of their life. May appear to be obsessive compulsive. They might re-check the front door several times before they leave in order to be sure they didn't forget to lock it.

* They get very upset when their routine is disturbed.

* Very intelligent and has developed a large number of creative methods for coping with their distractibility, memory or other problems. They may read an assignment into a tape recorder so they don't have to read it again. They replay it several times in order to remember the information.

* Others view them as extremely smart and have no idea of the amount of effort and frustration they endure.

* They may become extremely angry or upset but do <u>not</u> express it openly. Parents may have to analyze this child's behaviors more closely than their others because they are complicated, or "hard to read".

PART THREE

Adult

Categories

(Ages 17 and up)

Adult

Category I

(Classic)

Adult Category I

(Classic)

*** <u>Must</u> have met the criteria for one of the child or teen categories. Therefore, you must refer to Part One of this book.

* Very restless person. Always on the go.

* Involved in alcohol/drug abuse.

* Dropped out of school.

* Has many car accidents or traffic tickets.

* Has a very bad temper, but can be very charming.

* Has been arrested or involved with the court system for illegal activities.

* Has attempted suicide.

* Has seriously threatened violence against others.

* Changes jobs more often than others.

* <u>Overly</u> <u>active</u> sexually (promiscuous or very crude and blunt in their approach to sex. Very liberal and open to experimentation (more so than others).

* Divorced several times.

* Has numerous children with different partners. They may not have married these partners and they may have no contact with the children.

* Very manipulative.

* May physically abuse a spouse during a temper outburst and be remorseful afterwards.

Adult

Category II

(Semi-Classic)

Adult Category II

(Semi-Classic)

---

* Changes jobs often.

* Doesn't necessarily abuse alcohol/drugs but uses them more often than most people (ic: They drink beer or alcohol 3 or 4 times a week, even if they don't get drunk).

* Highly verbal, but can't carry on a two-way conversation in which they must listen and share. They seem to want control or attention.

* They've had a history of their current behavior. In other words, there was no dramatic "overnight" change in their personality or behavior.

* Dropped out of school.

* Trouble maintaining relationships. May have been divorced or separated several times.

* <u>Unusual</u> sex drive (over- or under-active).

* Has a bad temper but doesn't react physically.

* Not violent or aggressive criminal behaviors, but they do get more traffic tickets than most people.

* Loses car keys, house keys or papers often.

*   Although an adult, still seems immature and acts like a teenager.

*   Poor relationship with spouse due to impulsive decision making.

*   Isn't insightful to the needs of their children. When this topic is discussed in a formal setting, they can understand and see what they are doing wrong. However, their impulsiveness in an informal setting keeps them from performing.

*   They are often late for appointments or forget them.

*   Meets the criteria for one of the child or teen categories. To determine this, you must refer to Part One of this book.

Adult

Category III

(Semi-Complex)

Adult Category III

(Semi-Complex)

* Met the criteria for one of the child or teen categories.

* Doesn't change jobs often, but has to work harder (longer hours, for example) to accomplish their task.

* May be a quiet and subdued personality. They don't bounce off the wall or get overly excited.

* They take a great deal of time to make decisions.

* They are <u>overly</u> organized. They try to structure their environment in such a way that they are not faced with situations that require a quick response.

* Well liked by most people.

* Didn't drop out of school. In fact, made good grades, but had to put forth more effort and time than peers.

* Has a child or other family member (biological) who has ADD.

* Is adopted but little is known of biological parents.

* Has sought counseling (or thought about it) for "emotional" problems.

* Has anxiety attacks or phobias.

* Others (especially someone close to them) thinks they are depressed or have big mood changes.

* Any symptoms that are similar to ADD are attributed to bad "childhood experiences" (even though a <u>direct</u> connection cannot be explained).

* Other siblings, reared in the same environment, seem to have had fewer problems adjusting than they did.

* They have a niece or nephew that has ADD and are able to identify with them because of their experiences as a child.

* Write in any traits found in the child and teen categories that may apply to them <u>now</u>. (Because of the age, the traits may be somewhat different than when they were younger. ie: Instead of <u>forgetting</u> to turn in homework, they may forget other things.)

Adult

Category IV

(Complex)

Adult Category IV

(Complex)

* This is the most complicated category of all those listed. The ADD person in this category has either compensated for the symptoms of ADD or has avoided them in some way. Therefore, it will be necessary to examine their childhood and personal experiences very closely.

* They may have had enough money to avoid the problems encountered in holding a job or in managing their day to day life.

* They may own their own business which allows them to work at their own pace or to hire others to do what they have trouble doing.

* They may hold a position in a business that allows them to delegate responsibilities that they have trouble fulfilling.

* They may have been raised in a very strict and rigid manner that has helped them avoid making decisions and avoid the pitfalls that other ADD people have not been able to avoid.

* Only the person themself, knows that they have severe problems coping if they didn't adhere to their rigid way of life.

* Met the criteria for one of the child or teen categories.

* Financially successful in business.

* Any problems they have are unobservable to the outsider (ie: emotional or psychological problems).

* Extremely intelligent and verbal.

* They can recognize their short-comings and determine what it is they need to change. Because of this insight, they consult with a professional in a matter-of-fact manner. In other words, they do not appear to be "emotional wrecks".

* Their intelligence and creativity has allowed them to develop methods of compensating for the <u>Basic</u> ADD problems (ie: attention span, forgetting, distracted easily, etc.).

* They are extremely intelligent, but don't necessarily recognize it. They may feel just the opposite because of the effort and turmoil that <u>only</u> they know they have experienced.

* They may know more than the professional; in terms of the ability to analyze and think logically.

* They may have the same traits that exist in Categories I, II or III, but they are not observable to outsiders.

* They may appear to be "rationalizing" by a professional's definition. This is because he can explain, better than the professional, why he doesn't have some of the classic symptoms of ADD.

* Reviewing their childhood and teen years may be necessary before making a decision.

* In general, they were seen as very different from their peers; or, they felt as if they were very different.

* Has a child who has been diagnosed with ADD.

* Has a brother or sister who had learning problems. They may not have been formally diagnosed, but it was evident that problems existed.

* Has a parent, especially the father, who may fit some of the criteria for ADD (ie: alcohol abuse, losing jobs, reading problems, very active).

* Review the child and teen categories to determine which categories they might have fit (especially Category IV).

* Regardless of their "success" level, there is evidence of extreme intelligence within other family members.

* They are extremely talented in sports or in the arts (ie: music, drawing, singing, etc.).

* Strong religious faith that has helped them endure and cope.

Training

If you are interested in learning the complete evaluation process developed by Mr. Hunsucker, please note the following:

1. Training will be held <u>once</u> per year. It will be cancelled if the number of participants is low, or if there are too many participants from the same city.

2. Credentials are not important for attendance, but participants without a minimum of a masters degree will not be qualified to obtain future test materials from the companies that produce some of the tests.

3. Training will last 4 full days and attendance is required for <u>every</u> session.

4. Training will be scheduled each June or July (any changes will be reported to those interested in attending).

5. All materials will be provided.

For more information, please write:

Forresst Publishing
ADD Training
P. O. Box 155774
Fort Worth, Texas 76155

About the Author

Fact Sheet on Mr. Hunsucker

1. Has a Masters Degree in Psychology and 15 years experience in private practice.

2. Has been the administrator of a basic child care facility for troubled teens.

3. Provided testing and counseling for juvenile probation departments.

4. Provided testing and counseling for the Department of Human Services.

5. Provided testing and counseling for a state-sponsored teenage runaway program.

6. Created several ADD centers that provided testing and counseling for children, teens and adults with ADD.

7. Author of several books on ADD including the only one to become a best seller.

8. Named to Who's Who among Human Services professionals.

9. Named to Who's Who of the southwest.

10. Created the only comprehensive ADD evaluation procedure for children, teens and adults.